PEOPLE DID WHAT IN ANCIENT ROME?

I0802094

Shalini Vallepur

Crabtree Publishing Company

www.crabtreebooks.com

CRABTREE
PUBLISHING COMPANY
WWW.CRABTREEBOOKS.COM

Published in Canada
Crabtree Publishing
616 Welland Ave.
St. Catharines, Ontario
L2M 5V6

Published in the United States
Crabtree Publishing
PMB 59051
350 Fifth Avenue, 59th Floor
New York, New York 10118

Published in 2020 by Crabtree Publishing Company

Author: Shalini Vallepur

Editorial director: Kathy Middleton

Editors: Madeline Tyler, Petrice Custance

Design: Dan Scase

Proofreader: Wendy Scavuzzo

Production coordinator and prepress: Tammy McGarr

Print coordinator: Katherine Berti

All facts, statistics, web addresses and URLs in this book were verified as valid and accurate at time of writing.

No responsibility for any changes to external websites or references can be accepted by either the author or publisher.

Printed in the U.S.A./122019/CG20191101

All images are courtesy of Shutterstock.com, unless otherwise specified. With thanks to Getty Images, Thinkstock Photo and iStockphoto. Front Cover – zizi_mentos, Meilun, Macrovector, Alfmaler, VectorShow, matrioshka. 4&5 – Vasilius, Gaidamashchuk, Hennadii H, NotionPic, Peter Hermes Furian. 6&7 – Gilmanshin, Richard Mortel, miroslav110. 8&9 – Phant, MicroOne, Yuniar91, Kundra. 10&11 – Bahau, KittyVector. 12&13 – Miguel Hermoso Cuesta, WolfgangRieger, Miguel Hermoso Cuesta, NotionPic. 14&15 – TheBiblePeople, sailko, Joseph Calev, Shawn Hempel, topimages. 16&17 – mountainpix, Oligo22, Olivierw, Mike Cowlishaw, shakko. 18&19 – Costumes of All Nations (1882), eFesenko, Filippo Coarelli. 20&21 – antb, cge2010, Wayback Machine, mountainpix. 22&23 – A.Sych, adirekjob, Svietlieisha Olena. 24&25 – Krikkiat, Leigh Prather, clarst5, Moumou82. 26&27 – Lenorko, PetlinDmitry, khathar ranglak, Billion Photos, Ablakok. 28&29 – Babin, catinsyrup, picturepartners. Speech bubble – yana shypova. Background – Macrovector. Grapes – matrioshka. Scroll – Gaidamashchuk.

Library and Archives Canada Cataloguing in Publication

Title: People did what in ancient Rome? / Shalini Vallepur.
Names: Vallepur, Shalini, author.
Description: Series statement: People did what??? | Previously published: King's Lynn, Norfolk : BookLife Publishing, 2019. | Includes index.
Identifiers: Canadiana (print) 20190193085 | Canadiana (ebook) 20190193093 | ISBN 9780778774211 (hardcover) | ISBN 9780778774259 (softcover) | ISBN 9781427125118 (HTML)
Subjects: LCSH: Rome—Social life and customs—Juvenile literature. | LCSH: Rome—Civilization—Juvenile literature.
Classification: LCC DG78 .V35 2020 | DDC j937—dc23

Library of Congress Cataloging-in-Publication Data

CIP available at the Library of Congress

CONTENTS

Page 4 Welcome to Ancient Rome!
Page 6 The Roman Empire
Page 8 The Roman Colosseum
Page 10 The Gladiators
Page 12 Fresh Laundry at the Fullonica
Page 14 The Public Toilets
Page 16 Boys at School
Page 18 Girls at School?
Page 20 A Trip to the Baths
Page 22 Medicine and More
Page 24 Fine Dining
Page 26 Crime and Punishment
Page 28 Hair Care and Messy Makeup
Page 30 Learning More
Page 31 Glossary
Page 32 Index

Welcome to Ancient Rome!

Salve! That means "hello" in Latin—the language spoken in ancient Rome. When we talk about ancient Rome, we mean the time between the years 753 B.C.E. and 476 C.E. That's a long time!

To say "salve," say "sal-way."

THE ROMAN EMPIRE

After years of battling and expanding, ancient Rome grew to be a huge empire that stretched across parts of Europe, Africa, and Asia from 27 B.C.E. to 476 C.E.

KINGS, SENATORS, AND REPUBLICS

Ancient Rome started off as a small town and went through many changes. First, it was ruled by kings, but then ancient Rome became a **republic** in 509 B.C.E. During its time as a republic, a group of people called **senators** decided to expand Rome into an **empire** that was ruled by an emperor.

FACT
There had been seven kings before Rome became a republic..

Ancient Roman culture spread to other people around the empire, and they did some strange things! Let's take a look at some of the weird, wacky, and wonderful things that went on in ancient Rome and throughout the Roman Empire.

FACT
At its largest, the Roman Empire was home to around 65 million people.

The Roman Empire

When the Roman Empire began, Rome was ruled by emperors. The Roman emperor was the leader of Rome and the most important person around.

You're not special enough to wear purple.

The emperor was the only person who was allowed to wear the color purple. Purple clothes were hard to make because the dye was expensive.

If somebody else wore purple clothes, then they had to pay money as a punishment, or worse, they were killed!

CALIGULA DID WHAT?

Emperors did all sorts of crazy things. Caligula was the third emperor of Rome. He was popular with the people at first, but after an illness, he turned into a power-hungry emperor. He began acting very strange. He wanted everybody to treat him like a god and tried to make his horse a politician. Eventually, he was killed, to the joy of most people.

NERO DID WHAT?

Nero ruled between 54 C.E. and 68 C.E. During his rule, he killed his own mother and his wife. He also loved singing and performing, which most Romans thought was inappropriate for an emperor. Nero even instructed 5,000 soldiers to clap for him whenever he performed!

The Roman Colosseum

FACT
50,000 people could squeeze into the Colosseum.

Emperor Vespasian thought the Roman people deserved to be entertained after the crazy behavior of Emperor Nero. So he built the Colosseum in Rome. It was a huge amphitheater that was used to put on gladiator shows. The Colosseum opened in 80 C.E. with 100 days of gladiator and animal shows.

ANIMAL ANTICS

Crowds watched gladiators battle each other and animals. You might think that sounds a bit gross and gory, but people loved it. Here are a few of the animals gladiators fought at the Colosseum:

COLOSSEUM

FACT
Some species of animals nearly became extinct because the ancient Romans killed so many.

EVENTS AT THE COLOSSEUM

There were many different shows and events at the Colosseum. Executions were very popular. Criminals were often thrown into the Colosseum as a punishment, having to face all sorts of wild animals.

NAUMACHIAE

Naumachia shows were also very popular. Naumachia means "water battle" in Latin, and the shows were as spectacular as they sound. They usually happened on lakes, but the Colosseum put some on, too. The Colosseum was flooded with water and ships were brought in to recreate famous sea battles. Special boats with flat bottoms were made to fit inside the Colosseum!

The Gladiators

Most gladiators were criminals, prisoners, and enslaved people who were forced to train to fight as gladiators. Sometimes, tough gladiators became famous **celebrities** in Rome. Some Roman citizens became gladiators because they wanted to be famous.

Usually, a gladiator had to fight against another gladiator. Let's take a look at a few types of gladiators.

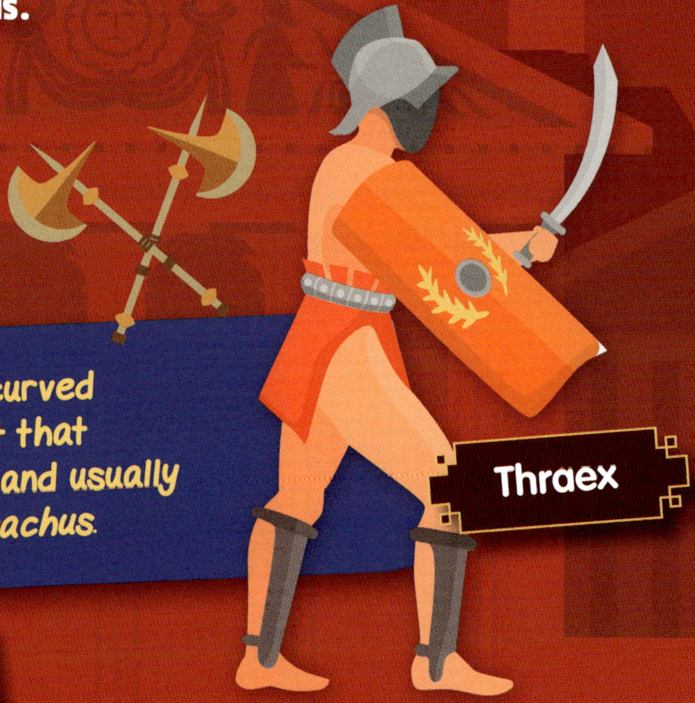

A *thraex* fought with a curved sword. He wore a helmet that covered his entire head and usually fought against a *hoplomachus*.

Thraex

So many different weapons and types of armor—what a thrill!

A *secutor* usually fought against a *retiarius*. The secutor wore a smooth helmet to make it harder for a retiarius to catch him with his net.

Secutor

A hoplomachus fought with a spear and usually carried a round shield. He was paired against a thraex in the Colosseum.

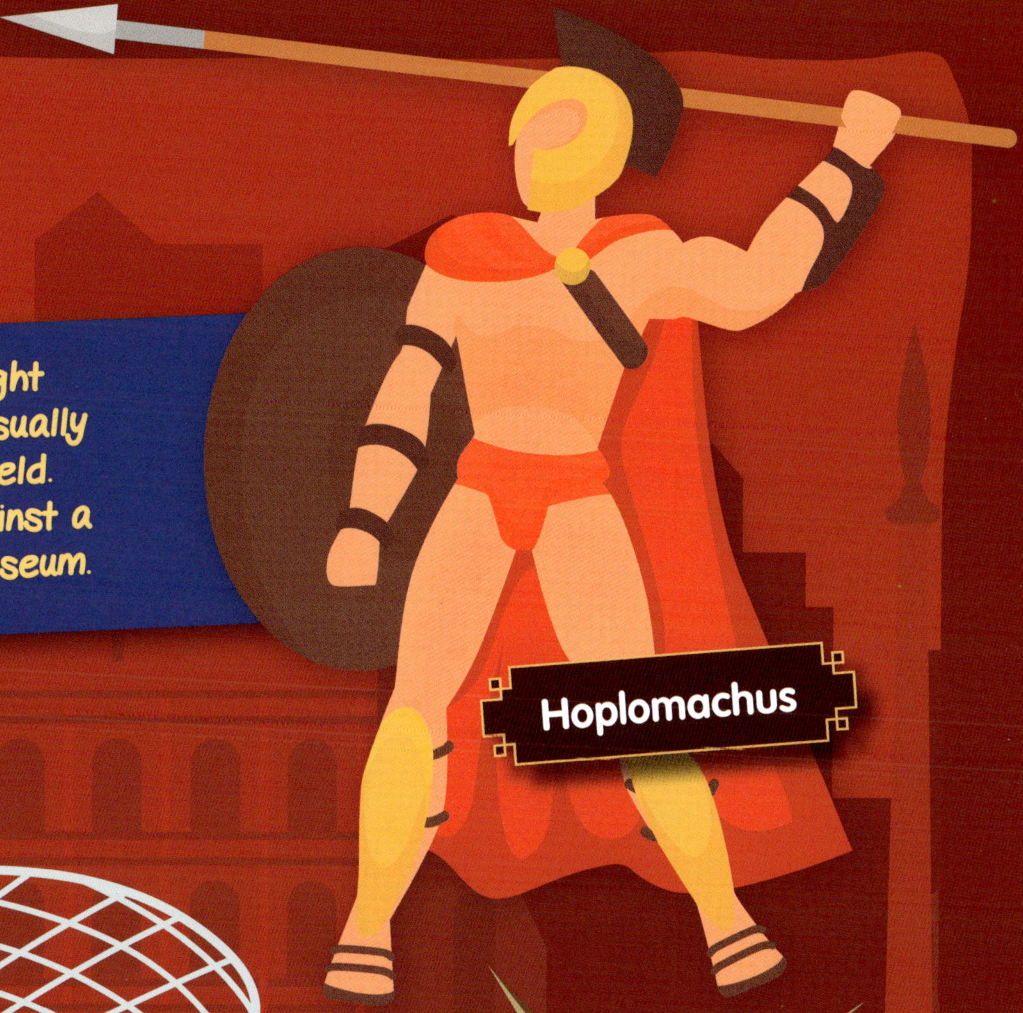

A retiarius barely wore any armor. Light on his feet, he fought with a sharp trident, or three-pronged spear. He used a net to trap his opponent.

Fresh Laundry at the Fullonica

THE PEE POTS

Tunics in ancient Greece were kept clean and fresh—but not with soap. The ancient Greeks used pee instead! Urine was very easy to find in ancient Rome. People placed little pots on street corners and soon enough, they were full of fresh pee.

Collecting pee pots

The pots were brought to a *fullonica*, the place where laundry was done. The pee was left to rest. It got smelly, but the liquid it became was perfect for washing clothes.

DO NOT TRY THIS AT HOME!

When it was ready, people called *fullones* mixed the pee with many different things, including clay and water. The smelly mixture was poured into a big pit.

BACK AT THE FULLONICA

STOMPING THE CLOTHES

The best part of the job was next. The fullones got into the pit and cleaned the clothes by stomping on them. The more they stomped, the cleaner the clothes became. The clothes were then rinsed off in water and hung up to dry.

The Public Toilets

Ancient Rome had its own sewer system, and there were around 100 public toilets. Public toilets were a great place to chat with a friend while doing your business.

Insert butt sponge here

FACT
Public toilets were made of marble and had pictures from Greek mythology on the walls. Fancy!

THE MIGHTY BUTT SPONGE

Butt sponge

THE DARK DEPTHS...

Poop, pee, and all things gassy—the public toilets seem like a funny place! But there was a dark side to the public toilets. The toilets were open to the rats and snakes living in the sewers below. When someone used a public toilet, they risked getting their butt nipped by a rat or whatever else was lurking below...

FORTUNA PROTECT US FROM GAS FIRE

The build-up of gases in the sewers sometimes led to fire. The gases caught fire, traveled up the sewer pipes, and burned any unfortunate butts! Luckily, Romans had the goddess Fortuna on their side. They painted her on the wall of the toilets, hoping she would protect them from snakes and gas fires.

Boys at School

Rich Roman boys usually started school when they were seven years old. If they were really rich, they stayed at home and were taught by tutors. Poor boys didn't go to school. They learned things at home and started working with their parents at an early age.

READING, WRITING, AND NUMERALS

Roman boys learned how to read and write at school. Math was important, too. They used a system of numbers called Roman numerals. Letters from the Latin alphabet were used instead of numbers. It was important that Roman boys could add and subtract, but Roman numerals could be quite long so it wasn't always easy.

1	I	11	XI	30	XXX
2	II	12	XII	40	XL
3	III	13	XIII	50	L
4	IV	14	XIV	60	LX
5	V	15	XV	70	LXX
6	VI	16	XVI	80	LXXX
7	VII	17	XVII	90	XC
8	VIII	18	XVIII	100	C
9	IX	19	XIX	500	D
10	X	20	XX	1000	M

SCHOOL TOOLS

To make math easier, children used an abacus. The abacus had little beads on it to count with, and it was small enough to carry around.

Schoolboys couldn't be trusted with expensive papyrus paper. They used tablets made of wax instead. Wax was put onto a wooden tablet and boys used a stylus to carve out letters and numerals.

Abacus

I WILL ALWAYS WATCH YOU

The school day started early and finished late. Schoolboys were followed to school by a *paedagogus*. The paedagogus was an enslaved person who made sure the boys behaved themselves. He watched the boys all day and if one of the boys dared to misbehave, the paedagogus would hold the boy down while the teacher whipped him.

Girls at School?

Girls didn't go to a school like the boys did. If they were rich enough, they were taught by tutors at home. Usually, girls were taught by their mothers or other women in the household. Just like poor boys, poor girls usually started working with their parents.

Girls were taught basic reading, writing, and math, the same as the boys. They also learned how to manage a household. Some girls grew up to have jobs, such as being a midwife or a dancer. However, most girls got married when they were just 12 years old, so most of their education was about learning how to be a good wife.

I love books about cleaning—said no one ever.

RUNNING THE ROMAN HOME

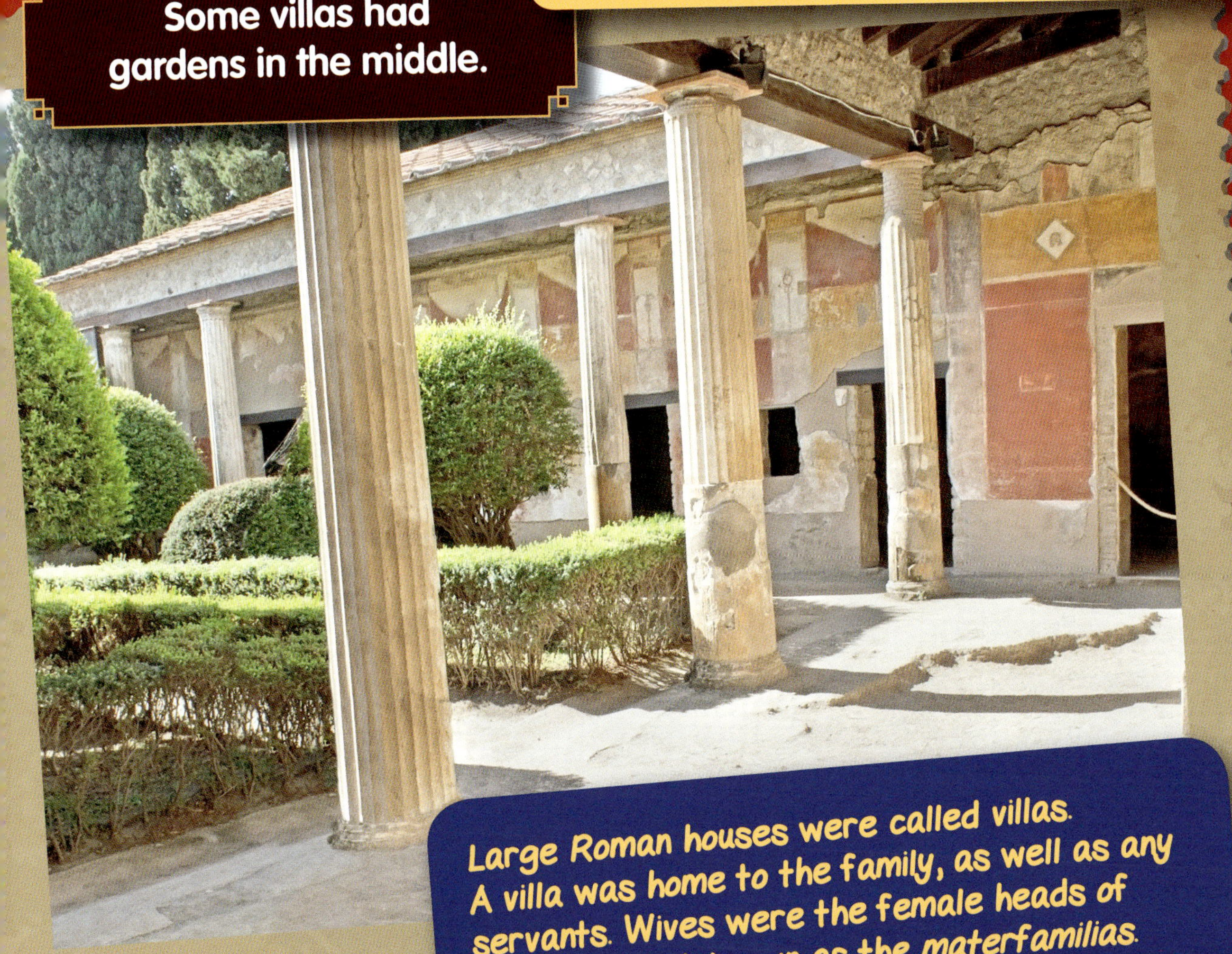

Some villas had gardens in the middle.

Large Roman houses were called villas. A villa was home to the family, as well as any servants. Wives were the female heads of the household, known as the *materfamilias*.

THE MATERFAMILIAS

It was up to the materfamilias to teach their children and run the household. The materfamilias also looked after the household money, so it was important they had a good math education.

A Trip to the Baths

The Roman baths in England

Staying clean was important to the ancient Romans, so they built public baths. The baths were social places, where people could meet their friends or do business deals. The baths were places of great beauty and relaxation. They were decorated with **mosaics** and grand statues.

FACT
In 300 C.E., there were around 900 baths across the Roman Empire.

AMAZING AQUEDUCTS

Aqueduct

How did Romans get water to the baths? They built aqueducts. Aqueducts carried water. Some aqueducts were great stone structures built across big fields and others were built underground as pipes. The water was heated up when it got to the baths.

FACT
Some aqueducts brought water into ancient Rome from 57 miles (92 km) away.

ENTER THE CALDARIUM

Strigil

The *caldarium* was a room in the baths where most of the washing took place. There was a hot bath in the center of the room and it got super steamy. Ancient Romans got really sweaty then scraped their dead skin away using metal strigils, or blades. The curved shape of the strigil was perfect for getting into nooks and crannies!

FACT
The caldarium was heated by pipes which carried hot water beneath the floor.

FREEZE IN THE FRIGIDARIUM

The frigidarium was the cold bath. People went there after the caldarium. The water there wasn't heated up, so it was perfect for cooling down. Follow that up with a massage and an ancient Roman was good to go!

Medicine and More

Pliny the Elder

WARTS AND ALL

Ancient Romans could treat just about anything. Pliny the Elder was a great **philosopher** who came up with cures for everyday problems. He suggested that burning cow poop to ashes and mixing it with honey could be a great fix for getting rid of pesky warts.

Being constipated is no fun, especially at a public toilet where everybody could see that you were struggling. Luckily, the ancient Romans had an amazing cure:

Step one: Mix wolf bile with a little bit of milk, salt, and honey.

Step two: Put the mixture on your belly button and wait a while.

Step three: Be free!

THE FIRST POOP

Fresh poop was thought to be a cure for many things. Thousands of people in ancient Rome had a disease called jaundice that made their skin look yellow. The cure was to take the first poop of a newborn donkey, mix it with wine, and drink it.

KISS THE MULE

Got hiccups? Pliny's cure was to put your lips against the nostrils of a mule. In other words, kiss the mule's nose! Headaches were easily cured, too. All you needed was an elephant to touch your head with its trunk. If the elephant sneezed, then it was a super cure.

Fine Dining

Rich Romans liked to throw big banquets to impress guests. The more food that was served, the richer and fancier the host was.

Glirarium

DORMICE ARE NICE

A dormouse is a type of mouse common in Europe. In ancient Rome, only rich hosts served them. The dormice were kept in a pot called a *glirarium*, where the mice would eat all day long. This made them plump and juicy when cooked. Yum!

BEAUTIFUL BAKED DORMICE

Step one: Mix ground pork with herbs and pine nuts.

Step two: Stuff the dormice with mince and then sew them up.

Step three: Cook in the oven.

Step four: Impress your guests!

Tiny, but tasty

THE TRICLINIUM

Dinner parties were held in the *triclinium*. That's the Latin word for "dining room." The triclinium was decorated with mosaics and paintings to impress the guests.

Ancient Romans set up sofas around their dining tables because they ate their meals lying down. Sofas were comfy and allowed everybody to reach the food on the table.

After dinner, the ancient Romans enjoyed entertainment. There were dancers or musicians playing the tuba or pipe organ. Bigger banquets had their own gladiator fights!

Crime and Punishment

THE TWELVE TABLES

The Twelve Tables was a set of laws that all ancient Romans had to follow. The laws were written on bronze tablets. If someone didn't follow the laws, they were punished. Today, people would find some of the laws a bit silly.

SOME ROMAN LAWS

People must not have meetings at night.

Women must not cry at funerals.

If a neighbor's tree leans into your farm, then you may remove the tree.

ROMAN CITIZENS

Roman citizens had many more **rights** than those who were not citizens. They also got easier punishments, and could even get away with certain crimes.

Things a Roman citizen could do:

- Wear a white toga
- Vote
- Become a politician
- Buy and sell goods

INTO THE SACK!

Some people have written about a punishment that sounds terrible. The criminal was put into a sack with a dog, a rooster, a snake, and a monkey. Then the sack was tied up and thrown into the sea!

BURIED ALIVE

Priestesses of the goddess Vesta had one job—to keep Rome safe. They did this by burning a fire in the temple. The fire had to burn all the time. If the fire went out or the priestesses broke other rules of the temple, they were buried in a small room in a big pit, with only a little bit of food and water, and left to die.

Hair Care and Messy Makeup

Roman beauty was no joke. Ancient Romans spent a lot of time on their appearance. They dyed and styled their hair. To dye gray hair, they mixed ashes, boiled walnut shells, and earthworms together and slathered it on their hair.

Roman women had hairpins and jewelry that were dipped in the blood of their favorite gladiators. If that wasn't enough, special face creams were sold that had gladiator sweat mixed in them!

THE FAIREST ONE OF ALL

A lot of women in ancient Rome wanted fair skin. They used products such as white chalk and white lead to make their faces pale. The only catch was that lead is poisonous. Using white lead on the face for a long time led to all sorts of horrible skin damage!

MEET IN THE MIDDLE

Dark eyelashes and dark eyebrows were all the rage for ancient Roman women. When something is burned, it leaves behind powdery black soot. This soot was applied to eyelashes and eyebrows to make them black. One big eyebrow, or a unibrow, was considered very fashionable.

LEARNING MORE

BOOKS

Malam, John. *Ancient Rome Inside Out.* Crabtree Publishing, 2017.

Nardo, Don. *Daily Life in Ancient Rome.* Heinemann, 2015.

Spilsbury, Louise. *Forensic Investigations of the Romans.* Crabtree Publishing, 2019.

WEBSITES

Visit this site for lots of cool pictures and facts about ancient Rome.
https://kids.kiddle.co/Roman_Empire

This site tells you all about the Colosseum.
www.dkfindout.com/us/history/ancient-rome/

Learn all about daily life in ancient Rome here.
www.historyforkids.net/ancient-rome.html

GLOSSARY

amphitheater An open, circular building for spectators to watch plays and sporting events

armor Metal coverings used to protect the body during battle

bile A yellow or greenish fluid in the stomach which helps to break down food

bronze A material made of copper and tin

celebrities People who are famous or in the public eye

constipated Having difficulty in passing poop

culture The way of life and traditions of a group of people

empire A group of countries or nations under one ruler

executions When people are killed as punishment

extinct Has no living members of its species

gladiator A man trained to fight other men or animals in an arena

jaundice A condition caused by the liver, in which the skin turns yellow

lead A poisonous chemical element sometimes found in paint

marble A hard form of limestone often used in sculpture and architecture

midwife A woman who helps other women during childbirth

mosaics Patterns or pictures that are made from small pieces of stone, tile, or glass

papyrus A material made from plants and used to write or paint on

philosopher A person who teaches or practices philosophy, or the study of thought

politician Someone who is involved in making government decisions

republic A place that is ruled by people who are voted into power by other people

rights Things a person is allowed to have or do

senators Members of a senate, or a governing group

sewer An underground area where waste goes

species A group of very similar animals or plants that can create young together

stylus An old tool used for writing which looked similar to a small, thin stick

temple A building in which people worship gods or goddesses

tunics Loose, knee-length shirts

INDEX

A

animals 7, 8, 9, 15, 16, 22, 24, 27

aqueducts 20

B

banquets 24–25

baths 20–21

beauty 28–29

boys 16–17

butt sponges 14–15

C

Caligula 7

citizens 10, 26

clothing 6, 12–13

Colosseum 8–11

cures 22–23

D

dormice 24

E

emperors 4, 6–7, 8

G

girls and women 18–19, 26, 28–29

gladiators 8, 10–11, 25, 28

L

laws 26

M

math 16, 17, 18, 19

mosaics 20, 25

N

Nero 7, 8

P

paedagogus 17

pee 12–13, 15

Pliny the Elder 22–23

poop 15, 22–23

public toilets 14–15, 22

punishments 6, 9, 26, 27

R

Roman Empire 4, 5, 6–7

Roman republic 4

S

school 16–18

V

Vespasian 8

villas 19